Through Th_ Go Round:

coincidences and synchronicities in the murder of John Lennon

D W Pryke

"On a river of sound
Thru the mirror go round,
round
I thought I could feel (feel,
feel, feel)
Music touching my soul,
something warm, sudden cold
The spirit dance was
unfolding..."

So sings John Lennon in #9Dream, knowing that Alice went through the looking glass into another reality, knowing that at the moment of death we all ride the merry-go-round ride through the mirror and beyond.

List of Contents:

Foreword.

For millions of people around the world, the death of John Lennon was one of the most shocking events of the last century, as high profile a murder as the assassination of J F Kennedy, and as incomprehensible an act as anyone could recall.

The killer was arrested within minutes of the shooting: in fact he made no attempt whatsoever to avoid capture, for he sat down on the sidewalk, took out a book, and calmly began to read.

Beforehand, he had set up a ritual arrangement of artefacts in his hotel room, knowing that the police would find them, exactly as he had left them. These items, photos, a music tape, documents, were perhaps meant to tell the world about his life, and tell the world that his life was over.

The murder of John Lennon was perhaps the surrogate suicide of Mark David Chapman.

Or, put another way, because he identified with the victim so strongly, in killing John Lennon, Mark David Chapman was symbolically killing himself.

So goes one theory.

But the full facts have never been revealed.

There was no trial; never a time when all of the facts were placed before the world's media for scrutiny.

And there was no funeral.

Yoko had the body cremated, apparently against John's wishes, and what became of the ashes remains unknown.

There was no "closure", and ordinary fans around the world were denied the real chance to grieve for their hero: they felt starved of information, and cheated of a proper farewell.

And so we have a number of other theories as to what happened and why: a number of alternate ideas have rushed in and multiplied to fill the vacuum.

Some believe Yoko had a hand in the murder of her husband. That she had conveniently given John's bodyguard and security advisor leave of absence, despite his insistence that security be increased. That she was having an affair with another man, and wanted John out of her life, and she had hired Mark Chapman, perhaps with CIA collusion, to kill him.

Some believe the US Government agencies, the FBI and the CIA saw John Lennon as a political threat, likely to arouse left wing activists in an anti-Carter campaign, and they therefore used Mark Chapman as a kind of "Manchurian Candidate" to kill the rock star.

Indeed, there are serious anomalies in the Mark Chapman story; serious questions that have never been answered, and we don't have all the data about his exact movements. And again, where there are gaps in our information, different hypotheses fill the vacuum.

Some believe there was at least one other Mark Chapman on the New York streets that night: that the others were deliberately planted to act as decoys, to confuse the overall picture as to Mark Chapman's movements.

Some believe John Lennon did not die.

Some believe that only days before, when he and Yoko had provided the New York police Department with a gift of bullet-proof vests, they had each kept a vest for themselves, and they were each wearing one of the vests that evening. The whole thing was an elaborate hoax to allow John Lennon to drop from public scrutiny.

Some believe John Lennon had been courting the idea of his own death for a long while. During the last year of his life, he had been having disturbing dreams of violent death, had had premonitions of his shooting, and was fascinated by the occult, by the idea of death and the afterlife. Some believe that he somehow secretly and subconsciously inspired his own death.

However, this book does not explore these different theories. After years of careful and meticulous research, I have pieced together what I think is a definitive account of what happened on December 8th 1980, and why.

***

My starting point is that Mark Chapman was a paranoid schizophrenic: disturbed, unstable but ever so convincingly normal to those who met him. He had been delusional from childhood, and had attempted suicide on at least two occasions. At the time of the murder, he was awaiting an appointment for psychiatric counselling.

He was certainly struggling to preserve his own tortured identity, but he was also planning to destroy another identity which he saw as a threat.

Or perhaps, more accurately, he was planning to kill another in order to preserve his own identity. I believe the two halves of that statement cannot be separated.

Understanding that is the key to understanding the murder.

This book explores the strange and tortured logic system that paranoid schizophrenics construct around themselves to justify their actions beyond any possible doubt. They build a meticulous and watertight fortress of ideas behind which they feel safe; they leave nothing to chance, and cement every last detail into place. They convince themselves that they are tuned to a special wavelength, so they hear and see and feel all around themselves images and signals and signs that only they can perceive and understand. Often they believe they have been chosen for a special act, a special mission to save the world.

For Mark Chapman, every thing around him could take on a special significance; every word of every song could be speaking to him, and only him; images on television could be beamed at him; the text of a book could be written especially for him; a painting could be sending him a secret, coded message.

Mark Chapman saw signs and signals and synchronicities at every turn - he heard the signs in the lyrics he listened to, saw signals in the album covers, and on television, in the paintings he collected, and in the books he read.

But that didn't make him a murderer.

There is another side to this complex equation – John Lennon.

This book proposes that Mark David Chapman and John Ono Lennon were slowly but surely coming together over a period of several years.

Fate, destiny, synchronicity or strange twists of coincidence were drawing them together,

Mark Chapman began to target John Lennon in 1979.

John Lennon had been incorporating images of death in his songs throughout his career.

**

This book explores the idea that there is a Fate or Destiny, or call it what you will, a force that somehow gives shape and form to existence.

It also explores that age-old adage that artistic, creative genius and madness are very close kin. John Lennon is on record as saying "I had a feeling I was either a genius or a madman. Now I know I wasn't a madman, so I must have been a genius."

And one point at which the madman and the genius can be said to overlap, is in their hyper-sensitivity to the force we call Fate or

11

Destiny. Their sub-conscious, their souls, are in tune to this something beyond.

This book proposes that on some strange and intangible subconscious level, John Lennon was indeed moving inexorably towards his own death. His lyrics, his album designs, his troubled dreams all reveal clues. At the same time, Mark Chapman, in his confused and troubled state of paranoid schizophrenia, had undergone a kind of three-way split, because he identified himself with both John Lennon and the fictional Holden Caulfield.

***

Mark Chapman was increasingly confused about his own identity. He felt he was losing his grip on his own personality, and was slowly becoming someone else. The person he most identified with was a fictional character: Holden Caulfield, from "The Catcher In The Rye". He had started re-reading the book during 1979, after almost collapsing on the sidewalk. It reminded him of the episode in "The Catcher" when Holden feels he is fading away into nothingness. As Mark Chapman read and re-read the book, he became convinced it had been written for him, about him.

He saw himself as the Holden Caulfield of his generation, destined to save the little children from harm: but then John Lennon, on his "Double Fantasy" album, was singing new songs claiming that he could send away the monsters and protect the children from harm. To Chapman, this sounded like John Lennon was claiming to be the new Holden Caulfield.

But if Mark Chapman was Holden Caulfield, John Lennon couldn't be Holden Caulfield too. And if Mark Chapman was John Lennon, then he couldn't be Holden Caulfield, too.

The problem was John Lennon.

Take John Lennon out of the equation, and Mark could fulfil his destiny and be Holden Caulfield. But taking John Lennon out of the equation would take a part of Mark Chapman out too, and that was dangerous. For Mark Chapman, it would be like killing a part of himself.

Holden Caulfield would be safe, but Mark Chapman or John Lennon would be harmed.

Killing John Lennon would be the suicide of part of Mark Chapman.

But if that could be done, then the Holden Caulfield part could live.

Such is the tortured logic of paranoid schizophrenia.

And the paranoid schizophrenic looks for answers. They construct an elaborate logic system to justify their every action, because they are convinced they are sane and normal. They look all around themselves, and they look closely at themselves. They analyse everything they do, trying to put into place a watertight, cast-iron logical justification and rationale for what they are feeling and doing. And because they feel suspicious and unsure of everyone around them, they look to themselves for the answers. That is why the mirror, or its symbolic representations, and in some cases even the metaphor of the mirror, is so vital: the mirrors they find all around them, show them who they really are.

In this way, the mirror becomes a vital in the search for their true identity.

For Chapman, suffering a crippling personality crisis, the mirror and its double images become a matter of his very survival. He clings to the mirrors he finds in songs, in album covers, in books and in works of art.

He hopes that peering into the mirror will tell him who he is, but the mirror can also reveal the dark side of his personality.

He thinks the face in the mirror is himself, but in reality, it is his reverse self.

In every culture, all over the world, there are myths and legends about the twin, the double or the rival bothers.

Castor and Pollux, Horus and Set, Cain and Abel, Tezcatlipoca and Quetzalcoatl.

In so many myths, the mirror double is associated with the darker side, with black magicians who use the mirror's surface to entrap their victims or to spy on them; with vampires, who have no reflected image because they are an undead double of a once living being; with shamans and shapeshifters who can become the double of another person...

Always, the mirror holds a special fascination and a special fear: it shows us another and intriguing side to reality, but it also shows us what we dread. In extreme cases, the mirror can show us both our past and our future – it can even show us our death.

"On a river of sound
Thru the mirror go round, round
I thought I could feel (feel, feel, feel)
Music touching my soul, something warm, sudden cold
The spirit dance was unfolding..."

So sings John Lennon in #9Dream, knowing that Alice went through the looking glass into another reality, knowing that at the moment of death we all ride the merry-go-round ride through the mirror and beyond.

***

John Lennon had bad dreams and nightmares about a violent death : he had had premonitions about his own death, and I maintain that #9 Dream was a recollection of one such 'dream-vision' or premonition.

John Lennon and Mark Chapman were the two spirits dancing so strange that John sings about in #9 Dream; Mark Chapman is the angel of destruction John Lennon sings about in "Help Me To Help Myself", one of his final lyrics.

#9 Dream

So long ago
Was it in a dream, was it just a dream?
I know, yes I know
Seemed so very real, it seemed so real to me
Took a walk down the street
Thru the heat whispered trees
I thought I could hear (hear, hear, hear)
Somebody call out my name, as it started to rain
Two spirits dancing so strange
Ah! böwakawa poussé, poussé
Ah! böwakawa poussé, poussé
Ah! böwakawa poussé, poussé
Dream, dream away
Magic in the air, was magic in the air?
I believe, yes I believe
More I cannot say, what more can I say?

On a river of sound
Thru the mirror go round, round
I thought I could feel (feel, feel, feel)
Music touching my soul, something warm, sudden cold
The spirit dance was unfolding
Ah! böwakawa poussé, poussé
Ah! böwakawa poussé, poussé
Ah! böwakawa poussé, poussé
Ah! böwakawa poussé, poussé
Ah! böwakawa poussé, poussé

The song "Help Me To Help Myself", recorded just before his murder, brings to the surface John Lennon's feeling that an "angel of destruction" was closing in on him.

There is also the suggestion that he is aware that there is this twin persona, there is the "me" and the "myself"…

He sings,

"Well I try so hard to stay alive
But the angel of destruction keeps on hounding me all around,
But I know, in my heart
That we never really parted....."

**

Just hours after being caught on photograph getting Lennon's autograph, Mark Chapman had murdered his so-called idol.

John Lennon had spent the evening at the Hit Factory recording studio, and returned to the Dakota apartments around 11.00 p.m. As he and Yoko stepped from the cab and made their way to the Dakota's entrance, Mark Chapman stepped out of the shadows.

"Mr. Lennon" he said quietly, and Lennon turned.

At that instant, there was a burst of sound as Chapman fired five bullets into the rock star.

He then calmly put the gun down and took a book out of his coat pocket, sat cross-legged on the sidewalk, and started to read.

What possessed Mark Chapman to kill John Lennon?

Why did he feel he was on a special mission to kill him?

What had drawn him to Lennon?

There has never been a public trial, and Mark's own silence about the murder and his motives have added to the mystery.

***

Receiving the Signals:

Chapman suffered delusions from his childhood, and in his early teens, heard voices that he attributed to "Little People" who lived in the walls of his bedroom. Later in life, his disturbed mental state led him to attempt suicide, and by early 1980, he was receiving psychiatric counselling for severe depression and was battling against paranoid schizophrenia.

There are typically two sides to paranoid schizophrenia: a feeling that you are losing control of who you are, and an awareness that all around you, there are clues and signs that could help you cope with your problems. Chapman desperately looked for signs that would help him, and when he found such signs, he clung to them with supreme determination.

As is typical with paranoid schizophrenics, Chapman became convinced that he was able to perceive and even receive signs and signals and messages that are hidden from the rest of us. Every thing around him could take on a special significance; every word of every song was speaking to him; images on television were aimed at him; the text of a book had been written especially for him. That was his state of mind in 1980.

And to the paranoid schizophrenic, these signals must be responded to - they cannot be ignored, even though the rest of the world chooses to do so, because they are vital to the survival of the persona. You ignore the signals at your peril. More than this, the paranoid schizophrenic comes to believe that he or she has been specially chosen to perform a seemingly miraculous task. Such individuals sometimes see themselves as a champion, even as a Saviour, someone who has been given a special signal and a special mission that can not only save themselves, but can change the whole world.

Mark Chapman saw signs and signals and synchronicities at every turn - he heard the signs in the lyrics he listened to, saw signals in the album covers, in film and on television, and in the books he read.

He found the words, the lyrics, the television images and works of art all immensely powerful and completely irresistible; they had such a strong influence over his personality that they "spoke" to him and told him he must rid the world of the phoney John Lennon. They were also so powerful that they transformed the brutal and bloody reality of the murder into a kind of fantasised fictional thriller which he had to act out.

Mark Chapman, in the early stages of paranoid schizophrenia, was a huge fan of the rock star Todd Rundgren, playing his albums constantly, learning the lyrics by heart. (Many paranoid schizophrenics are attracted to public figures, rock stars, film stars....because they are the people manipulating or dominating the media; they are the people sending out the signals...they are the people who must be followed and watched, waiting for the next signal they send out....)

Chapman was convinced the lyrics and the album covers contained signs for him; he felt the lyrics held an almost spiritual significance.

Significant Album Covers:

As far back as 1971, Mark was aware of the parallels between Rundgren and Lennon.

Lennon in the famous "Imagine" scene

"The Ballad of Todd Rundgren."(1971)

Like a send-up of the famous image of Lennon at his piano singing "Imagine" (also 1971) this album cover shows Todd sitting with a noose round his neck: that he must hang for a crime he has committed, or that he is about to kill himself. Chapman was fascinated by the ambiguity of the message: suicide or execution, but which was intended?

Also, Chapman noticed the alarming similarity with the image of John Lennon sitting at his piano playing "Imagine". It looked like Todd had intended this connection.

Over the intervening years, Chapman studied Todd's albums closely, looking for any clues that would confirm the message, especially any link with John Lennon. By late 1979, he was sure, and the message seemed totally clear - Lennon had had his chance to change the world with "Imagine": now he had to die.

"The Ballad of Todd Rundgren" was the album Mark left in his display at the Sheraton hotel when he checked out for the final time. As a statement, Chapman was declaring that Lennon had to die. The ideas of execution and suicide are still there, but by now perhaps they are confused: perhaps the killing of John Lennon should be seen as a kind of surrogate suicide. Chapman could not kill himself – he had tried as recently as the start of November 1980 – but he could kill the man whose mirror image he had become – John Lennon.

Because, Chapman knew about the mirror images and televisual signals he had been receiving for years. He understood them in minute detail.

Back in 1973, Todd was experimenting with mirror images and the idea of splitting personalities and multiple identities:

"A Wizard/A True Star" (1973)

On Todd's album, "A Wizard/A True Star", the front and back covers show a face splitting and breaking up into two, possibly three. Everything on the cover is breaking up and tumbling down, as if the universe is coming apart. The front and back covers are exact images of each other, continuing the mirror image theme. On the inside, the album opens out to show Todd in a mirror-tiled bathroom, surrounded by multiple split images. Again, the images are mirror reflections of each other, the right-hand inner sleeve exactly mirroring the left-hand inner sleeve.

The inner sleeve of "A Wizard/A True Star"

"Walls & Bridges" (1974)

Lennon himself uses similar ideas on his "Walls & Bridges" album of 1974, with its cover sliced into 3 fold-over strips that make composite and alternative pictures of Lennon's face.

It is a perfect example of the way Lennon played with these ideas. The album design is all about childhood, it includes paintings he did as a young schoolboy, and the fold-over strips to create different faces are an echo of the similar comic strip game of his childhood. But as always with John Lennon, his games have a serious side: one combination of the fold-over strips looks chillingly like a death mask.

On the album's inner sleeve, he is wearing multiple pairs of spectacles, as if offering a pun on seeing things clearly, and again he is playing with the idea of multiple appearances, multiple personalities.

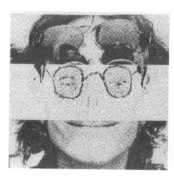 

In the "Todd" album of 1974, Todd Rundgren is beginning to experiment with the idea of broadcast signals and the idea that information, especially visual information, is made up of hundreds and thousands of tiny bits. This concept is explored again and again, by Todd, by Salvador Dali, by Lennon himself – in fact, it is the basis of television images and computer images.

With the "Todd" album, the inner sleeve contained a large computer generated image of Todd's face made up of hundreds of names from his fan-club directory, as if to acknowledge that without these thousands of fans, there would be no Todd.

Mark was devastated to find that his name was not part of the picture - it was as if Todd had ignored him. This was a devastating blow to Chapman, and for a while he was hurt and puzzled by Todd's apparent indifference.

To Chapman, it seemed that Todd was unaware of him. That Todd did not know who his Number One fan was.

It seemed to Chapman, that he didn't count, he was invisible – he was a nobody.

By 1976, and the "Faithful" album, Todd is openly parodying The Beatles' "White Album", even doing a 'faithful' cover version of Lennon's "Strawberry Fields".

"Faithful" (1976)

"White Album" (1968)

To Mark Chapman, the message was clear: Todd was not only mirroring John Lennon, but countering the creative force of the Beatles with his own genius.

In addition, Mark Chapman was aware that "The White Album" has other, more sinister associations: it is claimed that the Beatles' songs "Helter Skelter" and "Little Piggies" inspired Charles Manson to murder Sharon Tate, and others in 1969. Roman Polanski, Sharon Tate's husband, had used the Dakota apartments as a setting for his film "Rosemary's Baby", about a woman giving birth to the Devil's child.

When Chapman stood outside the Dakota on December 6th 1980, he was convinced Mia Farrow walked past him - and she had played the role of the mother in Polanski's film. Mark Chapman took this as another example of synchronicity, a sure sign he was in the right place, and it was the right time.

The television theme continued throughout Todd's career. On the cover of "Hermit of Mink Hollow" 1978, Todd stares out from a TV screen and Mark picks up the broadcast loud and clear. To

Chapman, it mirrors Lennon's "Imagine" album, where his face is fading in or fading out, because the signal is not yet at full strength. This idea of television and broadcast signals becomes a dominant feature of Todd's work over the next few years, and Mark Chapman waited eagerly for each new signal.

"The Hermit of Mink Hollow" (1978)

"Imagine" (1971)

Released in February 1980, the "Adventures In Utopia" album is all about television; it was intended to be launched alongside a television project Todd was working on. The record opens with a high-pitched test signal, the inner sleeve is designed to be a TV broadcast Test Card, complete with guidelines to make fine tuning adjustments. For Mark, the message was clear: the broadcast just needs a little fine-tuning; just hold on a while longer and the signal will become crystal clear.

"Adventures in Utopia" (February 1980)

And the main image on the front is of new life, or perhaps death: a silver cyberpod, or a sarcophagus floating in space. Together, the message was clear to Chapman: the time for fine tuning has come, and if you follow these messages, you can change the world and start everything over anew.

Chapman did not have to wait long for the final signal. By the end of the year, in November 1980, Todd has released his "Deface The Music" album. This whole album, the cover and the individual songs, is a parody of the "With The Beatles" album issued in 1963.

"Deface the Music" (1980)   "With The Beatles" (1963)

For Mark Chapman, here is Todd telling him, as clearly as he could, and just before the publicised issue of Lennon's "Double Fantasy" album, that The Beatles, and Lennon in particular, have to be "de-faced". The idea of death is so strong: the dead, eye-less faces on the marble busts, the sombre black and white of the design. This album triggered Mark to go to New York and commit the murder.

But Lennon too had been sending out signals for years. Even as a Beatle, Lennon had played with images of death and inserted cryptic clues into the albums: a whole myth has grown around the idea that Paul McCartney was killed in a car crash and a substitute band member had to be found. The Sgt. Pepper album is the graveside scene of Paul's funeral, "Abbey Road" shows the funeral procession of Priest (Lennon) Undertaker (Ringo) Corpse (Paul) and Gravedigger (George).

Perhaps his solo albums are more concerned with his own growth and development, rather than death. The 'primal scream' "Plastic Ono Band" album is about his traumatic childhood, though the cover shows he and Yoko lounging beneath an ancient oak tree, at peace at last; the "Rock'n'Roll" album cover shows him as a leather-jacketed adolescent, with blurred, ghost-like figures passing him in the street; "Walls & Bridges" has images and paintings from his schooldays, but the cover has fold-over strips that make up different faces, different personalities - and one combination makes a colourless, grinning death-mask; "Mind Games" seems to show him discovering a spiritual 'rock' in Yoko (she appears as a kind of Ayres Rock on the horizon) and "Imagine" shows him emerging as a solo artist - or fading as a Beatle.

The "Plastic Ono Band" album (1970) was about Lennon coming to terms with his traumatic childhood, and being abandoned by his parents. It opens a cycle of ideas and lyrics that Lennon effectively closes ten years later, with the songs on "Double Fantasy". For Mark, most noticeable was the idea of the child inside the adult/the adult inside the child, because he could identify strongly with that.

The tolling bell that begins the track called "Mother", seems to echo down the next ten years, being used by Todd Rundgren on his 1974 album "Todd", and again by Lennon on "Double Fantasy." This was no accident, but a deliberate feature Lennon incorporated into his work.

Ten years later, on "Double Fantasy", the opening track, "Starting Over" and the track "Beautiful Boy" both begin with the bell striking: Lennon is consciously completing the circle, for he has come to terms with his childhood and become a man, with a child of his own. A number of the lyrics deal with this idea of the child within the adult, and protecting the child from the big bad world and all its evil.

Mark Chapman heard the bell ringing as if it was the signal he had been waiting for: Todd had sung about "The bell in your head will ring..." in his song "All The Children Sing". It is a song about the end of the world, when all the pain and corruption and hatred are no more. It is a joyous day, a day of celebration, when all the children can sing because their world of pain is finished.

For Chapman, killing John Lennon would be his way of ridding the world of corruption and phoniness. The bell was summoning him to the murder, like Macbeth is drawn towards King Duncan's chamber.

Chapman also recognised other clues in the lyrics on "Double Fantasy", namely Lennon claiming he will protect the children from the monsters, the carousel turning round and round, like the one Phoebe rides on at the end of Catcher In The Rye....

It seemed that Lennon's lyrics were full of little clues to tie them in to "The Catcher" and to Todd's ideas of this world of phoniness and corruption has to end.

It was all coming together.

Significant Lyrics:

Mark Chapman threw himself into things to an excessive degree: he didn't just experiment with drugs, he became a high school "drug freak"; he wasn't simply intrigued by religion, he became a "Jesus Freak", he didn't just help in the Vietnamese refugee camps, he became a crusader for a better world for children. And he wasn't just a fan of Todd Rundgren, he idolised him.

Mark Chapman believed Todd's lyrics and music were special, in that they reflected everything he had experienced, everything he felt or thought. He learned the lyrics by heart and could sing all the various parts of the songs, even where Todd had laid down numerous tracks. He believed Todd's albums "spoke" to him, because they had a truly spiritual dimension.

As early as 1973, Chapman was already disillusioned by John Lennon, both as a Beatle and as a solo artist, and listened to Todd attacking him in the song titled "Rock and Roll Pussy" on the "A Wizard/A True Star" album.

Also of significance here is the song "Zen Archer", in which Todd sings of "oceans of tears/ life without death/ and death without reason" and the Zen archer steps out of the shadows to slay another victim. To Chapman, it seemed that Todd had foreseen the murder that had to come.

"To the promise kept and broken/ To the love that's never spoken/ Just as surely as I'm in your ears/ A dark figure slips from out of the shadow."

On the live 1974 album "Todd Rundgren's Utopia", he sings a track called "Freak Parade" in which he sings,

"I never was bothered by bad dreams/They never made me afraid/But then I never did dream I'd wake up/And find me in the freak parade."

"Todd" 1974

On the1974 "Todd" album , Mark Chapman was spellbound by three keys songs; "An Elpee's Worth of Toons" in which Todd screams "I want to Change the World", a sentiment that Mark Chapman was in tune with. Another significant song was "The Last Ride", which Chapman thought so beautiful that he later played it during his first suicide attempt on Hawaii. His idea was to die to the lyrics that had meant so much to him during his life.

And then, there is "A Dream Goes on Forever", in which he sings

"You're so long ago and so far away/ But my dream goes on forever/I guess I believe that I'll see you one day/ For without it there is no dream"

This combination of ideas was a potent mix. Dreams, wanting to change the world that was just one big "freak parade", and the figure slipping out of the shadows to kill another victim – all these will feature heavily later.

***

At the same time, John Lennon was singing his "#9 Dream", which, I am convinced, was a clear premonition of the murder.

#9 Dream

So long ago
Was it in a dream, was it just a
dream?
I know, yes I know
Seemed so very real, it seemed so
real to me

Took a walk down the street
Thru the heat whispered trees
I thought I could hear (hear, hear,
hear)
Somebody call out my name, as it
started to rain

Two spirits dancing so strange

Ah! böwakawa poussé, poussé
Ah! böwakawa poussé, poussé
Ah! böwakawa poussé, poussé

Dream, dream away
Magic in the air, was magic in the
air?
I believe, yes I believe
More I cannot say, what more can I
say?

On a river of sound
Thru the mirror go round, round
I thought I could feel (feel, feel, feel)
Music touching my soul, something
warm, sudden cold
The spirit dance was unfolding

Ah! böwakawa poussé, poussé
Ah! böwakawa poussé, poussé
Ah! böwakawa poussé, poussé

Ah! böwakawa poussé, poussé
Ah! böwakawa poussé, poussé
Ah! böwakawa poussé, poussé
Ah! böwakawa poussé, poussé
Ah! böwakawa poussé, poussé
Ah! böwakawa poussé, poussé
Ah! böwakawa poussé, poussé
Ah! böwakawa poussé, poussé

Lennon sings, "Was it in a dream? Was it just a dream?" because "It seemed so very real, it seemed so real to me.." and indeed, it was too real to be a dream. The song had come to Lennon in the middle of the night, words and music almost complete.

There are the "two spirits dancing so strange", two personalities drawn together – killer and victim. Then, a figure steps out in front of him and he hears "somebody call out my name (John, John, John....)" On the night of the murder, Chapman had stepped out of the shadows and quietly called, "Mr. Lennon."

It is a dream, and everything is coming together, and there is "magic in the air" because all this was unfolding like a scene from a film.

And then the shots are fired and there is "a river of sound," and then, when the explosion dies down, "music touching my soul, something warm, sudden cold," as the 5 bullets find their target and he starts to lose his grip on life.

Then, as Lennon slips "through the mirror go round, round" towards death, he is aware that "the spirit dance was unfolding...." and he is the spirits slowly drifting to the other side.

Lennon himself gave special significance to this song. In the very title he uses the number 9, his special, mystical, magical number.

***

Mark Chapman looked back on his time in the Fort Chaffee refugee camp as one of the happiest times in his life: he was protecting the children from further harm and helping them make a better world; he was regarded as a "Pied Piper" who the children followed, or a "Captain Nemo", full of despair and anger at the cruelties of an uncaring world.

1978 Hermit of Mink Hollow

This album has Todd's gaunt face staring out from a television screen. It is like a special broadcast, beamed directly to the listeners. The album's songs seemed to sum up his time at Fort Chaffee perfectly, with its lyrics about corruption, poverty and suffering, and loneliness - and a time coming when the world will end and everything will be changed for the better.

The lyrics of "All The Children Sing" reminded Chapman of the refugee camp, where he would play guitar and lead the children in song. But the lyrics are also about Judgement Day, when "the sun and moon collide/ Isn't gravity a funny thing? The Universe explodes apart? All the children sing." And the signal when this will happen, when this world will come to an end and a better world begin?

"A bell in your head will ring."

There are songs about being on the verge of breakdown, like "Out of Control" where Todd sings "I think I'm gonna explode / I think I'm going out of control". (Mark had attempted suicide in 1977 and was receiving psychiatric help)

There are songs like "Bag Lady" and "Bread" where the subject is poverty and children starving, and a callous, uncaring world.

"Can We Still Be Friends?" is about the problems of holding on to a relationship (Mark had recently cut all ties with Jessica, his long term girlfriend) To Mark, Todd was saying everything changes constantly and sometimes relationships will suffer - it's not a sign of failure, it's just a natural cycle, "it's time for the wheel to turn".

In "Too Far Gone" Todd sings about family break-up: "Why don't you write your mother?/ Why don't you call your family/ They're expecting an answer/ Spare them your strange behaviour..."

Mark Chapman was, above all else, a very lonely young man, so alone and with a life so incomplete, that he seemed desperate to find the missing other half of himself. For him, every line of every song on this album was full of meaning, and aimed specifically at him.

"Deface the Music", released late1980, continues Todd's theme of an evil, ugly world, where "scared little children run away" in fear, where the adults suffer unsatisfactory relationships. Many of the lyrics are questioning, challenging whether things really have to be this way...but there are no answers.

In "Where Does The World Go To Hide?" we hear about "All the people down here, they fight everywhere/ They destroy and they poison/ They don't even care/ So where does the world go to hide?"

In "Alone" Todd sings, "Nobody knows how lonely it can be/ And he was tired of being alone/ Alone, alone/ Nobody knows how lonely it can be/ And I'm so tired of being alone."

He asks, "Do you know the meaning of emptiness?", and sings

"There's an end to the fable/ Where does all this lead?/ That for everyone who needs someone/ There is someone there to need.."....

Mark Chapman knew the meaning of emptiness, and was searching for that someone who would make him feel complete.

That other person was the fictional Holden Caulfield, or the famous John Lennon.

But lyrics aside, the main impact of the album was to show to Mark Chapman that the Beatles, and their style of music, and Lennon in particular, were all to be "de-faced", or eliminated.

Double Fantasy was released mid November 1980, and immediately it gave Mark the signal he was waiting for: Todd had told him to listen for the bell in your head, and there it was, loud and clear on Lennon's new album.

For John Lennon, it signalled a new beginning, a "starting over" again, after five years of 'retirement'. This new bell also closes a ten year cycle that had begun with "Mother" on his Plastic Ono Band album.

For Mark Chapman, it was the signal he had been promised. It was the bell ringing in his head. It was time to end the old order of things and start anew.

The "Double Fantasy" album is like a dialogue in song between John Lennon and Yoko Ono, but the themes were instantly recognised by Mark Chapman. They sing of making the world a better place, especially for children, and in particular for their beautiful child. In the world of the album, children are safe and protected, and loved, a major theme in "The Catcher in the Rye".

But Mark Chapman saw himself as the protector of little children. He had been the "Pied Piper" at Fort Chaffee, with hordes of Vietnamese refugee children following him as he strummed his guitar and sang songs for them - Lennon was a phoney, an impostor, just posing for the cameras.

In "Beautiful Boy" the bell rings again, and they sing "Close your eyes/ Have no fear/ The monster's gone/ He's on the run and your daddy's here." In the song called "Clean-up Time" they sing there are "No rats aboard the magic ship/ Of perfect harmony.." because this is a perfect, magical, fairytale world, where "The gods are in the heavens/ The angels treat us well/ The oracle has spoken/ We cast the perfect spell."

In "Woman", John Lennon sings about "The little child inside the man" and in "Beautiful Boys" Yoko sings, in reply, "You're a beautiful boy/ With all your little ploys/ Your mind has changed the world/ And you're now forty years old." Again, Mark Chapman appreciated the importance of the child inside the adult: it was there in his reading of "The Catcher in the Rye", and there in his own life, in his own mind: the little child inside telling him to go through with the murder, the adult inside telling him not to.

Lennon also uses the image of the turning wheels of life, in "Watching the Wheels", which Mark Chapman read as a reference to the Carousel in Central Park, so again there is the clear tie-in with "The Catcher in the Rye", where Phoebe rides the Carousel near the end of the novel, watched over, protectively by Holden Caulfield.

To Mark Chapman, all these references were crystal clear and overwhelmingly powerful - they all pointed to "The Catcher in the Rye", and confirmed his feeling that he was the new "Catcher".

The recent release of "Help Me To Help Myself", recorded just before his murder, brings to the surface Lennon's feeling that an "angel of destruction" was closing in on him. He sings,

"Well I try so hard to stay alive,

But the angel of destruction keeps on hounding me all around,

But I know, in my heart

That we never really parted....."

Within days, this "angel of destruction" had taken his life.

***

The Influence of Television:

From the early 1970s, Chapman also began to be aware of "television" signals and signs in the album covers and lyrics of Todd Rundgren: most noticeably the haunting face of Todd stared out at him from a television screen on the "Hermit of Mink Hollow" album, as if telling him to stay tuned and watch his television set.

In a similar way, on "Imagine", Lennon's face was fading from sight, or else fading into sight. It seemed to show Lennon fading out as a Beatle, and fading in as a solo artist - either way, Mark Chapman was receiving the signal clearly.

At another point in his career, John Lennon had offered an image of himself made up of hundreds of "pixels" on the back of his "Plastic Ono Band" album. It is the equivalent of a television image made up of thousands of points of light. Here, the five year old Lennon gives us a picture of the innocence of childhood.

Except of course, this was the time in his life when John Lennon felt most abandoned by his parents: first his father had left him, then his mother left John with his Aunt Mimi.

The sweet innocence belies the trauma of rejection that so blighted John's childhood.

On Todd's "Adventures In Utopia" album, he listened to high-pitched coded signals and was fascinated by the album's inner sleeve, which was designed to be a television "testcard", and so help fine tune reception.

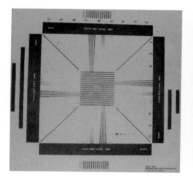 

A scanned image of Todd made up from the names of hundreds of fans seemed to be reflected in Salvador Dali's work with "Dalivision" (a clear pun on "television")

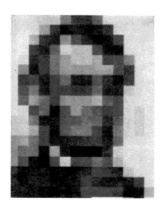

Dali's "Lincoln in Dalivision"

The importance of television signals becomes more important when we consider that John Lennon would watch television non-stop: Mark Chapman too, watched television day and night. On one occasion, during the summer of 1980, Chapman was convinced the message "Thou Shalt Not Kill" flashed across the screen. It was clearly aimed at him, and for a while, it stalled his plans to murder Lennon.

In response to it, he went back to reading the Bible, especially the Gospels of Saint John and Saint Mark. He was fascinated by the differences, by the apparent conflicting reports of these two accounts of the life of Jesus.

The Gospel according to Mark is all about casting out demons: the Gospel of Saint John is more about Jesus not knowing who he was, doubting his own identity, and coming to terms with the problems that caused him. Saint John versus Saint Mark.

It was corroboration that John and Mark would come face to face, and their battleground would be one of identity and demons.

When the signals first pointed to Lennon as the target, Mark Chapman researched what the rock star had been doing in the last few years. With rising anger, he read about Lennon's luxurious and reclusive lifestyle and phoney posturing in Anthony Fawcett's book One Day At A Time. The book gave him all the confirmation he needed - Lennon was a big phoney and deserved to die.

The most disturbing image in the book was that of John and Yoko hovering over the city, filling the sky in a black and menacing way, like evil giants or gods. To Chapman, it confirmed what John Lennon had become.

In the latter part of 1980, when John Lennon was beginning to launch the publicity for "Double Fantasy", Chapman was incensed to watch the rock star give a series of television interviews. By now, Chapman felt Lennon had to be his target, because he was everything that was phoney.

Here was a man who proclaimed his working class roots, enjoyed his street credibility, and yet he was one of the richest men in the world. He lived in great luxury, he bought whole container loads of luxury items, and yet wanted to be seen as an ordinary man.

The more he watched television, the more Chapman saw signs pointing him to New York. In late 1980, he watched a television adaptation of "Paul's Case" by Willa Cather.

It is the tale of a young man for whom the real world is mundane and dead, but the world of the theatre is alive and attractive. For a while, he lives a secret and double life, slipping away to work in the "real" world of the theatre. He then steals money and runs away to New York to live in luxury at the Waldorf-Astoria hotel, and when the law catches up with him, he commits suicide.

The programme inspired Chapman to follow suit.

There had always been something of the theatrical about Mark Chapman. As a teenager, he and a friend had gone to Chicago to make it big by playing in the bars of the city. They planned to play guitar and sing their own compositions, but after a couple of disastrous weeks, they had to admit defeat and return home.

At Fort Chaffee, Mark Chapman was a popular entertainer, singing around the camp fires, relaxed and confident.

There was always something of the dramatic too, about Mark Chapman. Everything had to be a big show, a major production. His suicide attempts were in this mould – the first an attempt to hook up a hosepipe to the exhaust, and go out listening to Todd Rundgren singing "The Last Ride"; the second, an attempt at the top of the Empire State Building, when he had put a gun to his head but couldn't pull the trigger. It was to be his final act, on the top of the Empire State Building – the biggest stage in the world.

Perhaps this is a real clue to why the murder happened: Chapman wanted the world to take note. He was going to kill the most famous man in the world – he would be in the headlines of every newspaper and every television report for days and weeks.

Through The Mirror Go Round by D W Pryke

Mark Chapman's Art Collection:

In the same way that television gave Chapman a visual stimulus to attach to, so did his collection of famous art works.

Mark Chapman began collecting particular works of art during 1979 and 1980, because in them, he recognised the signs and signals he had been searching for, and they gave him confirmation that he had been chosen to perform this special mission. These were powerful signals that could not be denied.

After marrying in 1979, Mark Chapman and his wife moved into a new apartment, and, in an effort to impress his in-laws, Chapman started collecting modern art. Soon, his interest became almost an obsession, and during late 1979 and the beginning of 1980 he spent hours looking through Library books and visiting the galleries on Hawaii. His first purchase was a Yamagata print of a Parisian street corner, because it reminded him of his visit to the French capital on his whirlwind world tour of the previous year.

Next, he borrowed money to buy a "Lincoln In Dalivision" by Salvador Dali.

"Lincoln In Dalivision" by Dali, 1976

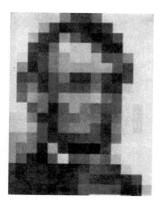

"Lincoln by Harmon" 1973

The image of Lincoln's face made up of different coloured "tiles" reminded Chapman of the face of Todd Rundgren on the scanned computer print-out, from the "Todd" album.

It was also similar to the face of the five year old John Lennon, made up of thousands of dots, on the back cover of the "Plastic Ono Band" album, and the grainy face of Todd Rundgren, staring at him from the TV screen, on "The Hermit of Mink Hollow" album cover.

In Chapman's mind, these images were connected, and they shared one thing: their composition meant that the image clarity was slightly obscured, as if the signal was not quite getting through. Now here was another face, or key elements of a face - that of Abraham Lincoln, and Dali had deliberately obscured all of the fine detail we normally look for in a face.

Chapman felt "The Hermit of Mink Hollow" had been telling him to wait for the next signal, and that it would come from a television screen, so he began to watch television all through the day and night, waiting and watching. But here was a message not on "television", but in "Dalivision", direct to him from one of the world's great modern masters. Chapman felt the link was overwhelmingly strong: the signal was trying to come through, but was still not fully clear, and he would have to watch and wait a little while longer.

Dali had based his composition on Harmon's experimental work on visual perception, and how little information we actually need to recognise a face: Dali extended the idea to make each 'tile' a separate image in itself, but the face of Abraham Lincoln is still clear.

Abraham Lincoln, or "Father Abe" was the patriarch of his nation, who believed he had been charged by God to bring the country together. He claimed to hear voices, and witnessed dreams and omens calling him to this special mission to become the Preserver of the Union - yet many believe he split the country in two, and in reality, he was the Sunderer of the Nation. He gave his famous "A House divided against itself cannot stand.." speech, and then watched his country torn apart by war.

He was assassinated, on Good Friday, while sitting in a theatre watching a play.

Perhaps, in all of that, Mark Chapman saw parallels between the "theatrical" killing of Lincoln and the "literary" killing of John Lennon, or the "theatrical" killing of Lincoln and his own attempt at a "theatrical" death.

Mark Chapman also borrowed money to buy Dali's print of "The Metamorphosis of Narcissus" because he was fascinated with the idea of reflections and mirror images. It shows Narcissus gazing into the mirror-like waters having fallen in love with his other self. He gazes in the water to find himself, but it leads to him losing himself. Again, the link with doubles and twin images is clear - Narcissus and his image; Mark Chapman and his other - John Lennon. (or Mark Chapman and Holden Caulfield.)

He borrowed more money to buy the Norman Rockwell print,
"Triple Self Portrait", seeing in it another expression of the power
of multiple selves and mirror images. This work introduces the
idea of the three-way split, and the internal battle. The warrior's
helmet perched on top of the easel signifies the battle within, the
conflict between the person we are, the person we would like to be,
the person we will become. Perhaps by this time, Mark Chapman
was aware of the triple personalities that dominated his life: John
Lennon, Holden Caulfield and himself.

That is why Chapman had to have this painting.

It is clear that, like the lyrics he knew by heart, and the album covers he saw as especially significant, these works of art were another way Chapman found to express the conflicts and confusions deep inside himself. He felt the artists were speaking directly to him, through their work, about the identity crisis he was experiencing.

The Influence of Books:

Mark Chapman was a very literary person: throughout his life he read widely.

One of the books that had an enormous significance in this case is Anthony Fawcett's "One Day At A Time", about the superstar lifestyle of John Lennon.

In October 1980, Lennon and Yoko Ono appeared on television promoting their new "Double Fantasy" album. Mark Chapman watched with growing contempt for a phoney superstar.

As a kind of follow-up, he borrowed Anthony Fawcett's book from the Library, and was angered at the luxurious lifestyle of Lennon, and at the apparent arrogance and phoniness of the star who was allegedly a "working class hero".

Chapman reacted to the photo of Lennon giving the victory sign beneath the Statue of Liberty, as if he will triumph in the coming struggle of identities. He was convinced that it must come to a life and death struggle between himself and Lennon, and that Lennon must die.

And there, on the inside front page, was a dark and brooding image of John Lennon and Yoko Ono, floating through the sky above a city, black and threatening like the Olympian god and goddess they had become, peering down on the world. For Chapman it was a chilling photograph - they are not just writing "Happy Birthday" across the sky, as Yoko had done for John's 40th birthday, now they have become evil presences dominating everything.

In another way, too, the image suggested death: that John Lennon and Yoko Ono are already spirits, already ghosts, already occupying their place in heaven.

The Catcher In The Rye:

From mid 1980, Mark Chapman was reading and re-reading "The Catcher In The Rye", a book he had first come across at college. He was so taken with the book, and the character of Holden Caulfield, he insisted his wife Gloria read it as well.

He was convinced the pages were speaking to him. He was sure he and Holden were two parts of the same whole: one a fictional and one a real side to a complex personality. He announced to Gloria, one day, that he intended to change his name to "Holden Caulfield".

In New York, Mark Chapman bought a copy of J.D.Salinger's "The Catcher In The Rye" and wrote in the front of it

"This is my statement.

Holden Caulfield - The Catcher in the Rye"

"The Catcher In The Rye" is a novel about adolescent aimlessness, and dissatisfaction with everything. Holden Caulfield, the main character, is disgusted with the phoniness of everyone he meets. The book describes a few days near Christmas, when Holden has been expelled from his school, and is wandering around New York, before going home to see his younger sister Phoebe. It deals with themes of teenage anxiety over sex, the feeling that everything is soiled, and innocence is lost. It is also, perhaps, for Holden, a journey back to childhood, when things were more simple.

The book takes its title, and its theme of being protective of little children, from the passage below:

"Anyway, I keep picturing all these little kids playing some game in this big field of rye and all. Thousands of little kids, and nobody's around - nobody big, I mean - except me. And I'm standing on the edge of some crazy cliff. What I have to do, I have to catch everybody if they start to go over the cliff - I mean if they're running and they don't look where they're going I have to come out from somewhere and catch them. That's all I'd do all day. I'd just be the catcher in the rye and all. I know it's crazy, but that's the only thing I'd really like to be. I know it's crazy."

Mark Chapman found countless links and coincidences in the book.

The timing:

"It was Monday and all, and pretty near Christmas, and all the stores were open. So it wasn't too bad walking on Fifth Avenue. It was fairly Christmasy. All those scraggy-looking Santa Clauses were standing on corners ringing those bells, and the Salvation Army girls, the ones that don't wear any lipstick or anything, were ringing bells, too."

The setting:

"They gave me this very crumby room, with nothing to look out of the window at except the other side of the hotel. I didn't care much. I was too depressed to care whether I had a good view or not."

"I didn't know then that the goddam hotel was full of perverts and morons. Screwballs all over the place."

The "fall" that Holden seems to be heading for, and that Mark Chapman seemed to be heading for:

"This fall I think you're riding for - it's a special kind of fall, a horrible kind. The man falling isn't permitted to feel or hear himself hit the bottom. He just keeps falling and falling."

And later:

"Anyway, I just kept walking and walking up Fifth Avenue, without any tie on or anything. Then all of a sudden, something very spooky started happening. Every time I came to the end of a block and stepped off the goddam kerb, I had this feeling that I'd never get to the other side of the street. I thought I'd just go down, down, down, and nobody'd ever see me again. Boy, it did scare me."

Which is exactly what happened to Mark Chapman in Hawaii.

Holden calls on the services of a prostitute, and again, Mark Chapman finds more synchronicity when he is visited by a prostitute in a similar green dress.

"She came in and took her coat off right away and sort of chucked it on the bed. She had on a green dress underneath. Then she sort of sat down sideways on the chair that went with the desk in the room and started jiggling her foot up and down."

Holden is shocked at the offensive graffiti he finds on the stairway: just like Mark Chapman discovers scrawled on the mirror in the apartments where he works as a security guard.

"But while I was sitting down, I saw something that drove me crazy. Somebody'd written '---- You' on the wall. It drove me damn near crazy. I thought how Phoebe and all the other little kids would see it, and how they'd wonder what the hell it meant, and then some dirty kid would tell them..."

And the image of innocent childhood at the end, with Phoebe riding the Carousel in Central Park:

"I felt so damn happy all of a sudden, the way old Phoebe kept going round and round. I was damn near bawling. I felt so damn happy, if you want to know the truth. I don't know why. It was just that she looked so damn nice, the way she kept going round and round, in her blue coat and all."

Mark Chapman believed the ink on the pages came alive when he read them - the very words were flowing through his veins, and he was living the story of Holden Caulfield, the Catcher in the rye, the protector of little children.

After shooting Lennon, Chapman got his copy of the book out of his pocket, sat down and started reading it once more.

Why "The Catcher In The Rye?"

In essence, "The Catcher In The Rye" is a story of a young man, alienated and alone, making a journey back home, to a more perfect past, to a time when his family were together and he felt loved. The setting is the capital city of the world, and winter, and freezing cold, because it is symbolic of the cold hard realities of big, bad the city as well as the harshness of Holden's present.

It is about feeling that you are not being understood, even though you have a vivid imagination and wonderful ideas, and even though you feel different, the world does not accept you. In fact, the world makes you feel different in a negative way, and you feel as though you don't fit in, you feel incapable of fitting in.

You get rejected, you are expelled from school, shunned by friends. The adults around you make you feel odd, even mad, and you feel isolated and lonely, so you wander through this cold, wintry landscape, going from bar to bar, looking for comfort or company, but nobody wants to know you. You end up feeling a nobody adrift in a cold, uncaring and violent world.

These are the feelings of adolescence, and that is what gives the book such a universal appeal to the young students who read it.

The book is also about reacting against authority, whether school or family, or the law. Again, you feel the whole world is against you, or you are against the whole world.

You are aware your family ties have changed; they are weaker or they are broken and you don't understand why or how. The family loved you in the past, but you have let them down, or they don't like the person you have become, and you are trying to restore that bond of former years, but it is impossible. The whole thing is doomed to failure, because it is idealistic and unattainable.

It is just as much a fantasy as the desire to turn your back on it all and run away to the backwoods and live a free and simple life without care, which is what Holden wants to do at the end of the book.

The story is about those adolescent problems of relating to others, especially the opposite sex, when you feel awkward, gauche, and clumsy. You are afraid of failure, and you try too hard, so that whatever you try comes out wrong, which just adds to your difficulties. It is about the way an adolescent young man has powerful emotions and feelings, but is afraid to show them, so he tries to hide them beneath a hard exterior, a protective layer of not caring or a layer of aggression and rebellion. Because that is safer, because feelings make you vulnerable and vulnerability brings possible pain and is seen as a sign of weakness, so all sensitivity is crushed, but really you are extraordinarily sensitive and you are feeling all kinds of agonies and nobody cares and nobody understands.

That is the appeal of the book, and especially to those who feel alienated from society and those who feel lonely and lost.

And feeling like that, they want to change the world! They want to make the world take notice of them! They have to do something, and the more dramatic the better, to force the world to sit up and recognise them!

****

Taken separately or singly, all these myriad signs and signals mean little, but to a paranoid schizophrenic like Mark Chapman, they are all tiny parts of a much larger whole. Like Todd Rundgren, like Harmon, like Dali, like Lennon himself, Chapman realised that the concept of information being made up of thousands of single parts all put together, is fundamental to our modern world. That is how a television screen displays its picture, in hundreds of lines; that is how a computer generates an image – in millions of pixels.

The paranoid schizophrenic is able to assemble and synthesise these signs. They are aware that each tiny piece is part of the whole, and they see the patterns that connect things together. Doing that is not just a game to them, it is vital to their very existence, because they believe without such a pattern or structure in their world, they simply cannot exist. Reality without a discernible structure would crush them.

Hence, they weave together the various signs and signals to create a complex and highly sophisticated structure or fabric, absolutely 100% watertight, made up of all the signals they are picking up. This structure is what gives substance to their life, this fabric is what gives them justification for their actions, and is what gives meaning to their perception of reality.

Once they have deciphered the signals and discerned the pattern in their life, they have to act on it. They have no choice – they have to complete what they see as their special mission, be it to save the world from evil, kill a cruel dictator or destroy a threat to themselves.

Chapman believed he was the receiver of signals that were demanding he rid the world of a phoney superstar who had deceived one generation and was just about to deceive another.

John Lennon was seen as a false "Catcher", an impostor who had to be stopped.

The Countdown to Murder

Mark Chapman is born in Fort Worth, Texas, on 10th May 1955

**

In 1969, Mark Chapman joins the YMCA South De Kalb branch. He is described as a "happy, well-adjusted boy."

But he is 14 and already showing signs of rebelling at home and at school.

He experiments with drugs: first marijuana and then LSD. He gets the reputation as a "garbage-head", someone who will take anything to get a high.

At this time, he runs away from home twice. He watches the Disney film "Toby Tyler" and emulates the main character by running away from home to join a circus.

**

In 1971, Mark Chapman discovers Jesus. He goes to an evangelist meetings led by the Reverend Arthur Blessed from California. Mark is overwhelmed. Friends notice a sudden and dramatic change in Mark.

**

By 1973, when he is 18, Mark's idol is Todd Rundgren. He listens to the albums constantly, learning the words by heart, and singing the backing tracks too.

His friends recall Mark as having an easy, relaxed manner with the girls. He is definitely not the classic loner of mis-conception.

In May 1973, Mark leaves home. He and a friend travel to Chicago, with the aim of playing in the clubs and making his fame and fortune as a comedian and songster.

But, the dream dissolved quickly and Mark returned a changed and disillusioned young man.

He applied for a job with the YMCA, working with children, and was accepted.

He is remembered as a charming young man, great with kids, and a great story-teller. The kids love him and call him Captain Nemo, from Jules Vernes' "Twenty Thousand Leagues Beneath The Sea."

**

In 1974, Mark is doing so well he is made Assistant Director of the summer camp, because he has shown considerable leadership qualities.

But…this bubble soon bursts, and Mark is back to square one.

**

In 1975, the YMCA launch a new ICCP/Abroad programme (International Camp Counsellor Programme) "to further international peace and understanding through person to person contacts in peace camps." Mark applies in February and is accepted on the programme.

His first choice venue is to be sent to the Soviet Union, and he enrols in a Russian language course in March at Georgia State University.

But, in mid June, Mark is sent to Beirut in the Lebanon. The highly volatile situation in Beirut explodes into violence only a few days after Mark's arrival, and he has to be evacuated back to the United States for his own safety.

Back in the States, Mark falls back on the YMCA for his next job, working in the camp at Fort Chaffee, Arkansas, which was a resettlement camp for Vietnamese refugees fleeing Saigon.

Again, briefly, Mark was in his element. But by December 1975, the number of refugees awaiting resettlement was so low that the Fort Chaffee camp was being run down.

Mark returns to Atlanta.

**

In January 1976, Mark enrols at Covenant College, a strict Presbyterian establishment in Tennessee.

Mark lasts just one semester.

By the summer of 1976, Mark is again looking for a job, and finds employment as an armed security guard. Friends notice a profound change coming over Mark.

**

Suddenly, in January 1977, Mark flies off to Hawaii.

He spends the first few months of the year enjoying a kind of extended holiday, but as his money began to run out, he grew increasingly depressed and suicidal.

By the summer, he has checked in to a private Hospital in Honolulu, and is receiving counselling for his suicidal feelings.

He drives out to the north of the island, puts a Todd Rundgren tape in the car, hooks a hose-pipe up to the exhaust and sits back to die, listening to Todd's "The Last Ride". But the hose-pipe is burnt through on the exhaust, and the suicide attempt comes to nothing. It leaves Mark angry with himself that he couldn't even kill himself.

He is then accepted as an outpatient at The Castle Memorial Hospital in Kailua. He is diagnosed with a severe depressive neurosis, but, strangely, he is released after only two weeks.

He stays at The Castle, though, getting a job as a maintenance worker, during the months of August to November.

In December 1977, his parents visit the island. They are on the verge of divorce, but put on a happy face for Mark. He shows them round the island and again enjoys a kind of extended holiday.

**

By summer of 1978, Mark has plans for another dramatic change: he intends to make a journey around the world. In July, Mark negotiates a loan from the Castle Hospital's credit union, and with the money he buys a ticket that will take him on a seven week tour to Seoul, Hong Kong, Singapore, Bangkok, Delhi, Israel, Geneva, London, Paris, Dublin, Atlanta and back to Honolulu.

Mark stays in YMCA hostels whenever he can.

The travel agent who had helped him make all the arrangement for this trip of a lifetime, is Gloria Abe, a half Japanese Yoko Ono look-alike, a demur and attractive young woman.

**

In January 1979, Mark proposes to Gloria.

They are married in June 1979, at the United Methodist Church in Kailua.

In August, under Mark's persuasion, Gloria changes jobs from Waters World Travel to the accounts department at The Castle Hospital.

Mark and Gloria move back to Honolulu, even though it was inconvenient for them both and meant a long commute to work, and they rent an expensive apartment.

In September 1979, Mark has a new passion – collecting works of art.

The increasing strain of making his marriage work, the rising debts because of his buying expensive paintings, and the lack of promotion at the apartment block where he works as a security guard, all contribute to Mark Chapman's problems in 1979.

By the end of the year, he has rowed with his employers and fallen out with his parents-in-law. More than ever, he feels trapped and alienated - more than ever he is not sure who he is or where he is going in life. Except, he feels he is on edge, waiting for a final signal that must surely come his way.

The Final Year:

By the end of 1979, John Lennon is thinking of getting back into the studio and recording again. Next Autumn, he will have finished the self-imposed five year period of looking after his son Sean.

**

In February 1980, Todd Rundgren releases "Adventures in Utopia", an album that has an inner cover design like television test cards, and an opening track that is a high-pitched signal. Mark Chapman is excited - is this what he has been waiting for? He listens to it over and over again, and decides the message is a "Wait and see", a call for him to adjust the fine tuning and just be patient.

By July 1980, Mark Chapman has real problems at work - there have been a spate of break-ins and he feels the others are blaming him for being sloppy and inefficient. In one apartment, the mirror has been scratched with obscenities and the family moving in are upset - especially the children. Mark feels he has let down the children, he has not been able to protect them from the evils of this world.

He is reminded of the scene in "The Catcher in the Rye" when Holden regrets not being able to protect his sister from the offensive graffiti. Mark buys a copy of the book and begins reading it.

Walking home one day from work, Mark feels faint and nauseous at the kerbside - again, he is reminded of the scene in the "Catcher" where Holden feels he is fading into nothingness.

**

John Lennon sails to Bermuda for a holiday. There, he works on the lyrics and arrangements for a number of songs planned for the new album. He visits a botanical garden and sees a beautiful flower called "Double Fantasy" and thinks that would be a wonderful title for the album - it is to be a joint venture with Yoko, and the songs will outline the loving relationship between the two of them.

**

By September 1980, Mark Chapman is alarmed at his own mental instability. He paints a picture of a sunset over Diamond Mountain and signs it "The Catcher in the Rye, Mark". He now identifies strongly with the hero of "The Catcher in the Rye" and tells his wife that he wants to change his name to Holden Caulfield.

In October, John Lennon and Yoko Ono appear on television to promote their forthcoming new album. They describe it as a "Heart Play", a dialogue of love between the two of them.

Mark Chapman watches with a cold detachment.

Amid the growing media interest in the new Lennon album, in October 1980 Esquire magazine features an article titled "John Lennon, Where Are You?", describing the rock superstar as a virtual recluse, frightened to leave his multi-million dollar apartment. It highlights the discrepancy between the so-called 'Working Class hero' and the multi- millionaire.

Mark Chapman reads the article with growing anger.

**

Chapman watches a television adaptation of "Paul's Case" by Willa Cather. It is the tale of a young man for whom the real world is mundane and dead, but the world of the theatre is alive and attractive. He steals money and runs away to New York to live in luxury at the Waldorf-Astoria hotel, and when the law catches up with him, he commits suicide.

Mark Chapman is inspired by the tale: he plans a trip to New York, and books a room at the Waldorf-Astoria. Not for the first time, Chapman has identified with a fictional character (at the age of 15 he ran away from home to join the circus, after watching the Disney film "Toby Tyler") He intends to re-enact the role of Paul, and go to New York - but also, he has identified with Holden Caulfield, who drifts around New York after being expelled from his High school. Mark Chapman is reading "The Catcher in the Rye" constantly, and he has insisted his wife reads it too - she tells him he reminds her of Holden.

Meanwhile, in response to the Esquire article, Mark Chapman researches John Lennon's life. From the Library, he takes Anthony Fawcett's "John Lennon: One Day At a Time". The book shows Lennon in his apartment, and Lennon and Yoko as dark figures in the sky over New York: Chapman is convinced that Lennon is an impostor and phoney. He is so angered by the image of Lennon that he openly talks of killing the rock star.

**

Mark Chapman signs out from his job as "John Lennon" then crosses out the name. He hears the new Lennon single "(Just Like) Starting Over" and hears the delicate chiming bell - this is the signal he has been waiting for.

On 29th October 1980, Mark Chapman flies to New York to confront John Lennon. He is armed.

He stays in the Waldorf-Astoria, and he walks to the Dakota Building. But, although he waits, he does not see John Lennon. With the gun in his pocket seemingly weighing more and more, he goes to the top of the Empire State building, takes out the gun and tries to kill himself. But he cannot do it, and he breaks down in tears. He knows there is a wicked little child inside himself, battling with the adult Mark, and the child is insisting he do something evil.

He flies back to Hawaii on 13th November.

In his book, "The Last Days of John Lennon," Fred Seaman, his personal secretary and chauffeur, states that Lennon was increasingly obsessed with astrology, numerology and had a morbid fascination with death. In the last months of 1980, John Lennon talked about death constantly, and what it felt like when you were shot.

"He said he dreamed of getting shot. He had nightmares of violent death - weird, recurring dreams, as he put it, about dying, about getting shot. He talked about getting shot as a modern form of crucifix - the best way of moving on to the next life with a clean Karmic slate."

On 17th November, "Double Fantasy" is released.

Mark Chapman listens in wonder at the lyrics. Not only is there the chiming bell, there is reference to "watching the wheels" of the Carousel (from the final scenes of "Catcher in the Rye") and songs about the child in the man, the man in the child. Lennon seems to be claiming that he will send all the monsters away and he will protect the children from harm - in other words, Lennon will be the new "Catcher in the Rye". Chapman feels these are the final pieces of the jigsaw: the synchronicity cannot be ignored.

Two days later, on 20th November, he is watching television, when the picture goes blank and "Thou Shalt Not Kill" appears across the screen. It is the sixth Commandment, as written in The Gospel of St. Mark - his Gospel, and Mark Chapman is shocked at the intensity of the experience, and sees it as an example of synchronicity, giving him a message to go back to reading the Bible. He does, looking closely at both The Gospel of St. Mark, and also The Gospel of St. John.

Mark's Gospel is the book of unclean spirits, about the house divided, about when Heaven and earth shall pass away - "And what I say unto you, I say unto all, Watch". Mark Chapman is reminded of the Abraham Lincoln connection (the "house divided" speech) and the lyrics of Todd Rundgren about the end of the world. The instruction to "Watch" seemed particularly apt, considering that Mark Chapman was watching television, waiting for a sign.

St. Mark's Gospel is all about casting out demons and being possessed: John's Gospel is all about identity, and how nobody knew Jesus, even those closest to him: even Mary at the end fails to recognise him. Both gospels together seem to present the two sides of his troubled personality, the identity crisis he is going through and the feeling he is possessed by evil spirits.

Saint Mark and Saint John in opposition.

For Mark Chapman, the message is clear: both he and John Lennon have their own Gospels, but the books are in opposition, are in conflict, presenting as they do, two very different pictures of Christ.

The opposition of himself and John Lennon is mirrored in the opposition of their two Gospels, and it confirms his feeling that Lennon is his doppelganger, and therefore he must be eliminated.

Increasingly depressed and troubled, and once again suicidal, Mark Chapman makes an appointment to see a counsellor at the Makiki Clinic - but not until 26th November.

On 22nd November, Todd Rundgren releases "Deface The Music" and Mark Chapman sees it as the final signal. He sees it as a clear denial of The Beatles and Lennon, and a call to him to deface their music and their influence.

Chapman signs himself off from his job as "John Lennon" and flies to New York a week later on his mission to kill this other John Lennon, this other "Catcher" who is an arch phoney.

He arrives in New York as "Holden Caulfield", and by now there is a three-way split that mirrors Norman Rockwell's "Triple Self Portrait" print: Mark Chapman, Holden Caulfield and John Lennon.

Mark Chapman stays at the West Side YMCA, where he watches ghostly figures on the broken television set in his room. Once again, he is struck by the symbolism of the moment: two ghost-like figures, himself and Lennon, are acting out their parts in this unfolding drama.

He stands outside the Dakota building and feels an overwhelming sense of deja vu, and then spots Mia Farrow walking by. She starred in the film "Rosemary's Baby", a film about a young woman impregnated by the Devil. The film was shot at the Dakota, and was directed by Roman Polanski, whose wife Sharon Tate was murdered by the notorious Manson family. They claimed inspiration for the killings came from the Beatles' "White album", and in particular, the tracks titled "Helter-Skelter" and "Piggies".

For Mark Chapman, this is another example of synchronicity, linking Lennon's songs to a fiendish murder and ideas of being possessed by the Devil.

Mark Chapman goes to a bookstore to buy a copy of The Catcher In The Rye but he is confronted by giant posters of Lennon, advertising his latest interview published in Playboy magazine. It seems to him that Lennon is everywhere, and that he has somehow replaced Holden Caulfield, that Lennon has become Holden Caulfield and therefore become the "Catcher".

When he eventually does buy a copy of Salinger's book, the next day, it is the last one on the shelf, and is beautifully bound in red. Again, Mark Chapman sees it as significant, as if that last book is meant to be his, and its red cover signifies the blood he must shed killing this phoney "Catcher".

Chapman wanders around Central Park and goes to the Carousel, which is featured in the final chapters of The Catcher In The Rye. He watches the Carousel going round and round, and is reminded that Lennon sings about "Watching the wheels go round.." on Double Fantasy.

While at the Carousel, Chapman catches sight of a girl in a red hat; it is just like in The Catcher in the Rye, where Holden is waiting to catch sight of his sister Phoebe wearing the red hunting hat she loved to wear.

He goes back to his hotel and calls for a prostitute to come to his room. He is amazed that when she appears, she is wearing a green dress, just like the prostitute who comes to Holden's room in The Catcher in the Rye.

This further synchronicity convinces Mark Chapman that he is the new "Catcher" and that his mission is to kill John Lennon, the phoney "Catcher".

Chapman arranges a "tableau" of important items in his hotel room. They include all the things that define who he is or who he was: photos from his happy days at Fort Chaffee; a tape of favourite Todd Rundgren songs; a still from "The Wizard of Oz" showing Dorothy comforting the Cowardly Lion; airline tickets; a copy of The Bible opened at John's Gospel, but changed to read "The Gospel according to John Lennon"...

Before he is satisfied with the final arrangement, he checks by entering the room a number of times, trying to see the items as the

Police will see them. He knows, when he leaves his hotel room that morning, he will never return.

This collection of items is like a grand suicide collage of items that have been important and significant in his life, and it is Chapman's way of signing himself off, of saying that the life of Mark David Chapman is over: it ends when the life of John Lennon ends.

THE END

Printed in Great Britain
by Amazon